The Life of Sir Thomas More

The Life of Sir Thomas More

by

William Roper

Templegate Publishers
Springfield, Illinois

© Templegate Publishers

Made and printed in the United States by
Templegate Publishers
302 East Adams Street
P.O. Box 5152
Springfield, Illinois 62705

ISBN 0-87243-118-5

ILLUSTRATIONS

All portraits in this book are the work of Hans Holbein. The portrait of Sir Thomas More on the cover is in the possesion of and copyrighted by the Frick Collection, New York; that of Erasmus by Caisse Nationale des Monuments Historiques; of the More Family by the Basel Gallery; of Dame Alice More by Lord Methuen. All other portraits are reproduced by gracious permission of Her Majesty Queen Elizabeth II.

Iudge More Sr Tho: Mores Father.

SIR JOHN MORE, father of Sir Thomas More in his 76th year

orasmuch as Sir Thomas More, Knight sometime Lord Chancellor of England, a man of singular virtue and of a clear unspotted conscience, (as witnesseth Erasmus), more pure and white than the whitest snow, and of such an angelical wit, as England, he saith, never had the like before, nor never shall again, universally, as well in the laws of our Realm (a study in effect able to occupy the whole life of a man) as in all other sciences, right well studied, was in his days accounted a man worthy famous memory; I William Roper (though most unworthy) his son-in-law by marriage of his eldest daughter, knowing no one man that of him and of his doings understood so much as myself for that I was continually resident in his house by the space of sixteen years and more, thought it therefore my part to set forth such matters touching his life as I could at this present call to remembrance. Among which very many notable things not meet to have been forgotten, through negligence and long continuance of

time, are slipped out of my mind. Yet to the intent the same shall not all utterly perish, I have at the desire of divers worshipful friends of mine, though very far from the grace and worthiness of them, nevertheless as far forth as my mean wit, memory and learning would serve me, declared so much thereof as in my poor judgment seemed worthy to be remembered.

This Sir Thomas More after he had been brought up in the Latin tongue at St. Anthony's in London, he was, by his father's procurement received into the house of the right reverend, wise and learned prelate Cardinal Morton, where (though he was young of years, yet) would he at Christmastide suddenly sometimes step in among the players, and never studying for the matter, make a part of his own there presently among them, which made the lookers-on more sport than all the players beside. In whose wit and towardness the Cardinal much delighting, would often say of him unto the nobles that divers times dined with him, "This child here waiting at the table, whosoever shall live to see it, will prove a marvellous man." Whereupon for his learning he placed him at Oxford, where when he was both in the Greek and Latin tongue sufficiently instructed, he was then for the study of the law of the Realm put to an Inn of the Chancery, called New Inn, where for his time, he very well prospered. And from thence was committed to Lincoln's Inn, with very small allowance, continuing there his study until he was made and accounted a worthy utter barrister. After this, to his great commendation, he read for a good space a public lecture of St. Augustine *de Civitate Dei* in the church of St. Laurence in the Old Jewry, whereunto there resorted Doctor Grocyn, an excellent cunning man, and all the chief learned of the city of London. Then was he made Reader of Furnival's Inn, so remaining by the space of three years and more. After which time he gave himself to devotion and prayer in the Charterhouse of London, religiously living there without vow about four years, until he re-

sorted to the house of one Mr. Colt, a gentleman of Essex that had oft invited him thither, having three daughters whose honest conversation and virtuous education provoked him there especially to set his affection. And albeit his mind most served him to the second daughter, for that he thought her the fairest and best favoured, yet when he considered that it would be both great grief and some shame also to the eldest to see her younger sister in marriage preferred before her, he then of a certain pity framed his fancy towards her, and soon after married her, nevertheless not discontinuing his study of the law at Lincoln's Inn, but applying still the same until he was called to the Bench, and had read twice, which is as often as any judge of the law doth read.

efore which time he had placed himself and his wife at Bucklesbury in London, where he had by her three daughters in virtue and learning brought up from their youth, whom he would often exhort to take virtue and learning for their meat, and play but for their sauce.

Who ere ever he had been reader in Court was in the latter time of King Henry the Seventh made a Burgess in the Parliament, wherein there were by the King demanded (as I have heard it reported) about three-fifteenths for the marriage of his eldest daughter, that then should be the Scottish Queen. At the last debating whereof he made such arguments and reasons there against, that the King's demands were thereby overthrown. So that one of the King's privy chamber, named Mr. Tyler, being present thereat, brought word to the King out of the Parliament house, that a beardless boy had disappointed all his purposes. Whereupon the King conceiving great indignation towards him could not be satisfied until he had some way revenged it. And forasmuch as he nothing having, nothing could lose, his grace devised a causeless quarrel against his Father, keeping him in the Tower until he had paid him an hundred pounds

fine. Shortly hereupon it fortuned that this Sir Thomas More coming in a suit to Dr. Fox, Bishop of Winchester, one of the King's privy council, they called him aside, and pretending great favour towards him, promised him that if he would be ruled by him, he would not fail but into the King's favour again to restore him, meaning, as it was after conjectured, to cause him thereby to confess his offence against the King, whereby his Highness might with better colour have occasion to revenge his displeasure against him. But when he came from the Bishop, he fell in communication with one Mr. Witford, his familiar friend, then chaplain to that Bishop and after a Father of Sion, and showed him what the Bishop had said unto him, desiring to have his advice therein, who for the passion of God prayed him in no wise to follow his counsel "for my Lord my Master (quoth he) to serve the King's turn will not stick to agree to his own father's death." So Sir Thomas More returned to the Bishop no more. And had not the King soon after died, he was determined to have

CECILY HERON, daughter of Thomas More, in her 20th year

gone over the sea, thinking that being in the King's indignation he could not live in England without great danger. After he was made one of the under-sheriffs of London, by which office and his learning together as I have heard him say, he gained without grief not so little as four hundred pounds by the year; since there was at that time in none of the Prince's courts of the laws of this realm any matter of importance in controversy wherein he was not with the one party of counsel. Of whom, for his learning, wisdom, and knowledge and experience, men had him in such estimation, that before he was come to the service of King Henry the Eighth, at the suit and instance of the English Merchants, he was, by the King's consent, made twice Ambassador in certain great causes between them and the Merchants of the Stilliard, whose wise and discreet dealing therein to his high commendation, coming to the King's understanding, provoking his Highness to cause Cardinal Wolsey (then Lord Chancellor) to procure him to his service. And albeit the Cardinal according to the King's request earnestly travailed with him therefore, among many other his persuasions alleging unto him, how dear his service must needs be unto his Majesty, which could not of his honour with less than he should yearly lose thereby seem to recompense him, yet he, loath to change his estate, made such means to the King by the Cardinal to the contrary, that his Grace for that time was well satisfied.

ow happened there after this a great ship of his that then was Pope to arrive at Southampton, which the King claiming for a forfeiture, the Pope's Ambassador by suit unto his Grace obtained, that he might for his Master the Pope have counsel learned in the Laws of this realm, and the matter in his own presence (being himself a singular civilian) in some public place to be openly heard and discussed. At which time there could none of our law be found so meet to be of counsel with this Ambassador as Sir Thomas More, who could report to the Ambassador in Latin all the reasons and arguments by the learned counsel on both sides alleged. Upon this the Councillors on either party in presence of the Lord Chancellor, and other the judges in the Star Chamber, had audience accordingly. Where Sir Thomas More not only declared to the Ambassador the whole effect of all their opinions, but also in defence on the Pope's side argued so learnedly himself, that both was the foresaid forfeiture to the Pope restored, and himself among all the hearers, for his upright and commendable demeanour therein, so greatly renowned, that for no entreaty would the King from henceforth be induced any longer to forbear his service. At whose first entry thereunto he made him Master of the Requests, having then no better room void, and within a month after, knight and one of his Privy Council, and so from time to time was by the Prince advanced, continuing in his singular favour and trusty service twenty years and above, a good part whereof used the King upon holidays, when he had done his own devotions to send for him into his private room, and there some time in matters of Astronomy, Geometry, Divinity, and such other Faculties, and some time in his worldly affairs, to sit and confer with him, and other whiles would he in the night have him up into the leads, there to consider with him the diversities, courses, motions, and operations of the stars and planets. And because he was of a pleasant disposition, it pleased the King and Queen, after the Council had supped, at the time of their supper for their pleasure commonly to call for him, and to be merry with them. When he perceived so much in his talk to delight, that he could not once in a month get leave to go home to his wife and children (whose company he most desired) and to be absent from the Court two days together, but that he should be thither sent for again, he much misliking this restraint of liberty, began thereupon somewhat to dissemble his nature, and so by little and little from his former mirth to disuse himself, that he was of them from thenceforth no more so ordinarily sent for. Then died one Mr. Weston, Treasurer of the Exchequer, whose office after his death the King of his own offer, without any asking, freely gave unto Sir Thomas More.

In the fourteenth year of his Grace's Reign was there a Parliament holden, whereof Sir Thomas More was chosen Speaker, who being very loath to take that Room upon him, made an oration, not now extant, to the King's Highness for his discharge thereof. Whereunto when the King would not consent, he spake unto his Grace in form following: "Since I perceive (most redoubted sovereign) that it standeth not with your Highness' pleasure to reform this election, and cause it to be changed, but have, by the mouth of the Right Reverend Father in God the Legate your Highness' Chancellor, thereunto given your most royal consent, and have of your benignity determined, far above that I may bear, to enable me, and for this office to repute me meet, rather than ye should seem to impute unto your Commons that they had unmeetly chosen, I am therefore, and

always shall be, ready obediently to conform myself to the accomplishment of your high commandment. In my most humble wise beseeching your most noble Majesty, that I may, with your Grace's favour, before I farther enter thereunto, make mine humble intercession unto your Highness for two lowly petitions, the one privately concerning myself, the other the whole assembly of your Common House. And for myself (Gracious Sovereign) that if it mishap me in anything hereafter, that is in the behalf of your Commons in your high presence to be declared, to mistake my message, and for lack of good utterance by me misrehearsed, to pervert or impair the prudent instructions, that it may then like your most noble Majesty of your abundant grace, with the eye of your accustomed pity, to pardon my simplicity, giving me leave again to repair to the Common House, and there to confer with them, and to take their substantial advice, what thing, and in what wise I shall on their behalf utter and speak before your noble Grace: to the intent their prudent advices and affairs be not by my simpleness and folly hindered or impaired. Which thing if it should so hap, as it were well likely to mishap in me (if your Grace's benignity relieved not my oversight) it could not fail to be, during my life, a perpetual grudge and heaviness to my heart. The help and remedy whereof in manner aforesaid remembered, is (most Gracious Sovereign) my first lowly suit and humble petition unto your most noble Grace. Mine other humble request, most excellent Prince, is this. Forasmuch as there be of your Commons here, by your high commandment assembled for your Parliament, a great number which are after the accustomed manner appointed in the Common House to treat and advise of the common affairs among themselves apart: and albeit (my liege Lord) that, according to your prudent advice, by your honourable writs everywhere declared, there hath been as due diligence used in sending up to your Highness' Court of Parliament the most discreet persons out of every quarter, that men could esteem meet thereto, whereby it is not to be doubted but that there is a very substantial assembly of right wise and politic persons: yet (most victorious Prince) since among so many wise men, neither is every man wise alike, nor among so many men like well witted, every man like well spoken; and if often happeneth, that likewise as much folly is uttered with painted polished speeches, so many boisterous and rude in language see deep indeed, and give right substantial counsel: and since also in matters of great importance the mind is often so occupied in the matter, that a man rather studieth what to say, than how; by what reason whereof the wisest man and best spoken in a country fortuneth among, while his mind is fervent on the matter, somewhat to speak in such wise, as he would afterward wish to have been uttered otherwise, and yet no worse will had when he spake it, than he hath when he would so gladly change it: Therefore (most Gracious Sovereign) considering that in all your high Courts of Parliament is nothing entreated but of matters of weight and importance concerning

your Realm, and your own Royal estate, it could not fail to let and put to silence from the giving of their advice and counsel many of your discreet Commons [except they] were utterly discharged of all doubt and fear how anything that should happen them to speak, should happen of your Highness to be taken: and in this point your well-known benignity putteth every man in right good hope. Yet such is the weight of the matter, such is the reverend dread that the timorous hearts of your natural subjects conceive towards your high Majesty (our most redoubted King and undoubted Sovereign) that they cannot in this point find themselves satisfied, except your gracious bounty herein declared put away the scruple of their timorous minds, and animate and encourage them out of doubt. It may therefore like your most abundant Grace (our most gracious King) to give to all your Commons here assembled your most gracious licence and pardon freely, without doubt of your dreadful displeasure, every man to discharge his conscience, and boldly in everything incident among, declare his advice, and whatsoever happeneth any man to say, it may like your noble Majesty of your inestimable goodness to take all in good part, interpreting every man's words, how uncunningly soever they be couched, to proceed yet of a good zeal towards the profit of your Realm and honour of your Royal person, the prosperous estate and preservation whereof (most excellent Sovereign) is the thing which we all your most humble loving subjects, according to the most bounden duty of our natural allegiance, most highly desired and pray for."

At this Parliament Cardinal Wolsey found himself much grieved with the Burgesses thereof, for that nothing was so soon done or spoken therein, but that it was immediately blown abroad in every alehouse. It fortuned at that Parliament a very great subsidy to be demanded, which the Cardinal fearing it would not pass the Common House, determined for the furtherance thereof, to be there present himself; before whose coming after long

debating there, whether it were better
but with a few of his Lords (as the
most opinion of the house was) or
with a whole train royally to receive
him there amongst them, "Masters,"
quoth Sir Thomas More, "forasmuch
as my Lord Cardinal lately, you note
well, laid to our charge the lightness
of our tongues for things uttered out
of this house, it shall not be amiss in
my mind to receive him with all his
pomp, with his maces, his pillars, his
pollaxes, his crosses, his hat, and
great seal too; to the intent that if he
find the like fault with us hereafter,
we may be the bolder from ourselves
to lay the blame upon those that his
Grace bringeth with him." Whereunto the House wholly agreeing, he was
received accordingly. Where after he
had in a solemn oration by many reasons proved how necessary it was the
demands there moved to be granted,
and further said that less would not
serve the King's purpose; he seeing
the company still silent, and thereunto nothing answering, and contrary to his expectation showing in
themselves towards his requests no
towardness of inclination, said unto

JOHN MORE, son of Thomas More, in his 19th year

them: "Masters, ye have many wise
and learned men among you, and
seeing I am from the King's own person sent hither unto you for the preservation of yourselves and all the
Realm, I think it meet you give me a
reasonable answer." Whereat every
man holding his peace, then began he
to speak to one Mr. Marney, who
making him no answer neither, he
severally asked the same question of
divers others accounted the wisest of
the company. To whom when none
of them all would give so much as
one word, being before agreed, as the
custom was, by their speaker to
make answer: "Masters," quoth the
Cardinal, "unless it be the manner of
your house (as of likelihood it is) in
such causes to utter your minds by
the mouth of your speaker, whom ye
have chosen for trusty and wise (as
indeed he is) here is without doubt a
marvellous obstinate silence;" and
thereupon required the answer of
Mr. Speaker, who reverently upon
his knees excusing the silence of the
house, abashed at the presence of so
noble a personage, able to amaze the
wisest and best learned in a realm,

and after by many reasons proving, that for them to make answer was it neither expedient, nor agreeable with the ancient liberty of the House; in conclusion for himself showed, that though they had all with their voices trusted him, yet except every of them could put into his own head all their several wits, he alone in so weighty a matter was unmeet to make his Grace answer, whereupon the Cardinal displeased with Sir Thomas More, that had not in this Parliament in all things satisfied his desire, suddenly arose and departed: and after the Parliament ended, uttered unto him all his griefs, saying, "Would to God you had been at Rome, Mr. More, when I made you Speaker." "Your Grace not offended, so would I too, my Lord," quoth he, and to wind such quarrels out of the Cardinal's head, he began to talk of that gallery at Hampton Court, wherewith so wisely brake he off the Cardinal's displeasant talk, the Cardinal at that present, as it seemed, wist not what more to say to him, but for revengement of his displeasure counselled the King to send him Ambassador into

Spain, commending unto his Highness his wisdom, learning and meetness for that voyage, and the difficulty of the cause considered, none was there so well able, he said, to serve his Grace therein.

Which when the King had broken to Sir Thomas More, and that he had declared unto his Grace, how unfit a journey it was for him, the nature of the country and disposition of his complexion so disagreeing together, that he should never be likely to do his Grace acceptable service therein, knowing right well that if his Grace sent him thither, he should send him to his grave; but showing himself nevertheless ready according to his duty, albeit with the loss of his life, to fulfil his Grace's pleasure therein, the King allowing well his answer, said unto him, "It is not our meaning, Mr. More, to do you hurt, but to do you good we would be glad. We therefore for this purpose will devise upon some other, and employ your service otherwise." And such entire favour did the King bear him, that he made him Chancellor of the Duchy of Lancaster, upon the death of Sir Richard Winfield, who had that office before. And for the pleasure he took in his company, would his Grace suddenly sometimes come home to his house at Chelsea to be merry with him, whither on a time unlooked for he came to dinner, and after dinner in a fair garden of his walked with him by the space of an hour holding his arm about his neck. As soon as his Grace was gone, I rejoicing, told Sir Thomas More, how happy he was, whom the King had so familiarly entertained, as I had never seen him do to any before, except Cardinal Wolsey, whom I saw his Grace once walk with arm in arm. "I thank our Lord, son," quoth he, "I find his Grace my very good lord indeed, and I do believe he doth as singularly favour me as any subject within this Realm. Howbeit (son Roper) I may tell thee, I have no cause to be proud thereof. For if my head would win him a castle in France (for then there was wars between us) it should not fail to go."

This Sir Thomas More, among all other his virtues, was of such meekness, that if it had fortuned him with any learned man resorting to him from Oxford, Cambridge, or elsewhere, as there did divers, some for the desire of his acquaintance, some for the famous report of his learning and wisdom, and some for suits of the Universities, to have entered into argument, wherein few were comparable to him, and so far to have discoursed with them therein, that he might perceive they could not, without some inconvenience, hold out much further disputation against him: then, least he should discomfort them, as he that sought not his own glory, but rather would seem conquered than to discourage students in their studies, ever showing himself more desirous to learn than to teach, would he by some witty device courteously break off into some other matters and give over. Of whom for his wisdom and learning had the King such an opinion, that at such time as he attended upon his Highness, taking his progress either to Oxford or Cambridge, where he was received with very eloquent orations, his Grace would always assign him (as one that was most prompt, and ready therein) *ex tempore* to make answer thereunto; whose manner was, whensoever he had any occasion, either here or beyond the sea to be in any University, not only to be present at the reading and disputations there commonly used, but also learnedly to dispute among them himself. Who being Chancellor of the Duchy, was made ambassador twice; joined in commission with Cardinal Wolsey once to the Emperor Charles into Flanders, the other time to the French King into France.

Not long after this the Water Bailiff of London (sometime his servant) hearing, where he had been at dinner, certain merchants liberally to rail against his old master, waxed so discontented therewith, that he hastily came to him, and told him what he had heard: "and were I, Sir" (quoth he) "in such favour and authority with my Prince as you are, such men surely should not be suffered so villainously and falsely to mis-report and slander me. Wherefore I would wish you to call them before you, and, to their shame, for their lewd malice to punish them." Who smiling upon him said, "Mr. Water Bailiff, would you have me punish them by whom I receive more benefit than by you all that be my friends? Let them a God's name speak as lewdly as they list of me, and shoot never so many arrows at me, so long as they do not hit me, what am I the worse? But if they should once hit me, then would it a little trouble me: howbeit, I trust, by God's help, there shall none of them all be able once to touch me. I have more cause, Mr. Water Bailiff (I assure thee) to pity them, than to be angry with them." Such fruitful communication had he oftentimes with his familiar friends.

o on a time walking along the Thames side with me at Chelsea, in talking of other things, he said to me, "Now would to God, son Roper, upon condition three

things were well established in Christendom I were put in a sack, and here presently cast into the Thames." "What great things be these, Sir," quoth I, "that should move you so to wish?" "Wouldest thou know, son Roper, what they be?" quoth he. "Yea marry, Sir, with a good will if it please you," quoth I. "I faith, they be these, son," quoth he. "The first is, that whereas the most part of Christian princes be at mortal wars, they were at universal peace. The second, that where the Church of Christ is at this present sore afflicted with many heresies and errors, it were well settled in an uniformity of religion. The third, that where the King's matter of his marriage is now come into question, it were to the glory of God and quietness of all parties brought to a good conclusion:" whereby, as I could gather, he judged, that otherwise it would be a disturbance to a great part of Christendom.

Thus did it by his doings throughout the whole course of his life appear, that all his travails and pains, without respect of earthly commodities, either to himself or any of his, were only upon the service of God, the Prince and the Realm, wholly bestowed and employed; whom in his latter time I heard to say, that he never asked of the King himself the value of one penny. As Sir Thomas More's custom was daily, if he were at home, besides his private prayers with his children, to say the seven psalms, litany, and suffrages following, was his guise nightly, before he went to bed, with his wife, children, and household to go to his chapel, and there upon his knees ordinarily to say certain psalms and collects with them: and because he was desirous for godly purposes some time to be solitary, and sequester himself from worldly company; a good distance from his mansion house builded he a place, called the new building, wherein was a chapel, a library, and a gallery, in which as his use was upon other days to occupy himself in prayer and study together, so on the Fridays there usually continued he from morning unto evening, spending his time duly in devout prayers, and spiritual exercises; and to provoke his wife and children to the desire of heavenly things, he would sometimes use these words unto them. "It is now no mastery for you children to go to heaven. For everybody giveth you good counsel, everybody giveth you good example. You see virtue rewarded, and vice punished, so that you are carried up to heaven even by the chins. But if you live in the time, that no man will give you good counsel, nor no man will give you good example, when you shall see virtue punished, and vice rewarded, if you will then stand fast, and firmly stick to God upon pain of life, if you be but half good, God will allow you for whole good." If his wife or any of his children had been diseased, or troubled, he would say to them, " We may not look at our pleasure to go to heaven in feather beds, it is not the way. For our Lord himself went thither with

great pain, and by many tribulations, which is the path wherein he walked thither, and the servant may not look to be in better case than his Master." And as he would in this sort persuade them to take their troubles patiently, so would he in like case teach them to withstand the devil and his temptations, valiantly saying, "Whosoever will mark the devil and his temptations shall find him therein much like to an ape. For as an ape not well looked to will be busy and bold to do shrewd turns, and contrariwise being spied will suddenly leap back and adventure no farther: so the devil, seeing a man idle, slothful, and without resistance ready to receive his temptations, waxeth so hardy that he will not fail still to continue with him, until to his purpose he hath brought him: but on the other side, if he see a man with diligence present to prevent and withstand his temptations, he waxeth so weary, that in conclusion he forsaketh him. For as much as the devil by disposition is a spirit of nature so envious, that he feareth any more to assault him, lest that he should thereby not only catch a foul

ANN CRESACRE (or GRISACRE), betrothed to John More, in her 15th year

fall himself, but also minister to the
man more matter of merit." Thus de-
lighted he evermore not only in virtuous exercises to be occupied himself,
but also to exhort his wife, and children, and household to embrace and
follow the same.

To whom for his notable
virtue and godliness God
showed, as he seemed, a
manifest miraculous to-
ken of his special favour
towards him, at such time as my wife
(as many others that year were) was
sick of the sweating sickness, who ly-
ing in so great extremity of that dis-
ease, as by no invention or devices,
that physicians in such case commonly use (of whom she had divers,
both expert, wise, and well learned,
then continually attendant upon her)
she could be kept from sleep: so that
both physicians and all others de-
spaired her health and recovery, and
gave her over: her father (as he that
most entirely tendered her) being in
no small heaviness for her, by prayer
at God his hands sought to get remedy, whereupon after his usual manner going up into his new lodging,

there in his chapel upon his knees with tears most devoutly besought Almighty God, that it would be like his goodness, unto whom nothing was impossible, if it were his blessed will, at his mediation to vouchsafe graciously to hear his petition; where incontinent came into his mind, that a glister should be the only way to help her, which when he had told the physicians, they by-and-by confessed, that if there were any hope of health, that it was the very best help indeed, much marvelling of themselves, that they had not afore remembered it. Then it was immediately ministered unto her sleeping, which she could by no means have been brought unto waking, and albeit after she was thereby thoroughly awaked, God's marks, evident undoubted token of death, plainly appeared upon her, yet she (contrary to all their expectation) was (as it was thought) by her father's fervent prayer miraculously recovered, and at length again to perfect health restored, whom if it had pleased God at that time to have taken to his mercy, her father said he would never have meddled with worldly matters after.

ow while Sir Thomas More was Chancellor of the Duchy, the See of Rome chanced to be void, which was cause of much trouble. For Cardinal Wolsey, a man very ambitious, and desirous (as good hope, and likelihood he had) to aspire unto that dignity, perceiving himself of his expectation disappointed by means of the Emperor Charles, so highly commending one Cardinal Adrian, sometime his schoolmaster, to the Cardinals of Rome, in the time of their election for his virtue and worthiness, that thereupon was he chosen Pope, who from Spain (where he was then resident) coming on foot to Rome, before his entry into that city did put off his hose and shoes, barefooted and barelegged passing through the streets towards his palace with such humbleness, that all the people had him in great reverence. Cardinal Wolsey waxed so woe therewith, that he studied to invent all ways of revengement of his grief against the Emperor, which as it was the beginning of a la-

mentable tragedy, so some part thereof not impertinent to my present purpose I reckoned requisite here to put in remembrance. This Cardinal therefore, not ignorant of the King's unconstant and mutable disposition, soon inclined to withdraw his devotion from his own most noble and virtuous wife Queen Katherine, aunt to the Emperor, upon every light occasion; and upon other, to her in nobility, wisdom, virtue, favour and beauty far incomparable to fix his affection, meaning to make his so light disposition an instrument to bring about this his ungodly intent, devised to allure the King (then already contrary to his mind nothing less looking for than falling in love with the Lady Anne Bullen) to cast fancy to one of the French Sisters, which thing, because of enmity and war was at that time between the French King and the Emperor (whom, for the cause afore remembered, he mortally maligned) he was desirous to procure, and for the better achieving thereof requested Langland, Bishop of Lincoln, and ghostly father to the King, to put a scruple into the King's head, that it

was not lawful for him to marry his
brother's wife; which the King not
sorry to hear of, opened it first to Sir
Thomas More, whose counsel he required therein, showing him certain
places of Scripture, that somewhat
seemed to serve his appetite, which
when he had perused, and thereupon, as one that never had pro-
fessed the study of Divinity himself,
excused to be unmeet many ways to
meddle with such matters; the King,
not satisfied with this answer, so sore
still pressed upon him, therefore, in
conclusion he condescended to his
Grace his motion, and further, that
the matter was of such importance as
needed good advice and deliberation,
he besought his Grace of sufficient respect advisedly to consider of it;
wherewith the King well contented
said unto him; Tunstall and Clarke,
Bishops of Durham and Bath, with
other learned of his Privy Council
should also be dealers therein. So Sir
Thomas More departing, conferred
those places of Scripture with the ex-
position of divers of the old holy doctors, and at his coming to the Court,
in talking with his Grace of the fore-

said matter, he said, "To be plain
with your Grace, neither my Lord of
Durham, nor my Lord of Bath,
though I know them both to be wise,
virtuous, and learned, and honourable prelates, nor myself with the rest
of your Council, being all your
Grace's own servants, for your manifold benefits daily bestowed on us, so
most bounden unto you, be in my
judgment meet counsellors for your
Grace herein; but if your Grace
minds to understand the truth, such
counsellors may you have devised, as
neither for respect of their own
worldly commodity, nor for fear of
your princely authority, will be inclined to deceive you."

To whom he named St. Je-
rome, St. Augustine, and
divers other holy doc-
tors, both Greeks and
Latins: and moreover
showed him what authority he had
gathered out of them, which although the King did not very well
like of (as disagreeable to his Grace's
desire), yet were they by Sir Thomas
More (who in all his communication
with the King in that matter had al-

ways most wisely behaved himself)
so wisely tempered, that he both
presently took them in good part,
and oftentimes had thereof conference with him again. After this were
there certain questions proposed
among his Council, whether the King
needed, in this case, to have any
scruple at all, and if he had, what
way were best to deliver him of it?
the most part of whom were of the
opinion, that there was good cause,
and that, for discharging of it, suit
were meet to be made to the See of
Rome, where the King, hoping by
liberality to obtain his purpose,
wherein (as after it appeared) he was
far deceived, then was there, for the
trial and examination of this matrimony, procured from Rome a Commission, in which Cardinal Cam-
pegines and Cardinal Wolsey were
joined Commissioners, who, for the
determination thereof, sat at the
Blackfriars in London. Where a libel
was put in for the admitting of the
said matrimony, alleging the said
marriage between the King and the
Queen to be unlawful, and, for proof
of the marriage to be lawful, was

there brought in a dispensation; in which, after divers disputations thereupon holden, there appeared an imperfection, which by an instrument or brief, upon search found in the treasury of Spain, and sent to the Commissioners into England, was supplied, and so should judgment have been given by the Pope accordingly, had not the King, upon intelligence thereof, before the same judgment, appealed to the next general Council. After whose appellation the Cardinal upon that matter sat no longer.

It fortuned before the matter of the said matrimony brought in question, when I, in talk with Sir Thomas More, of a certain joy commended unto him the happy estate of this realm, that had so catholic a Prince, that no heretic durst show his face, so virtuous and learned a clergy, so grave and sound a nobility, so loving and obedient subjects, all in one faith agreeing together: "True it is indeed (son Roper)," quoth he, and in commending all degrees and estates of the same

went far beyond me, "and yet (son Roper) I pray God," said he, "that some of us, as high as we seem to sit upon the mountains, treading heretics under our feet like ants, live not the day, that we gladly would wish to be at league and composition with them, to let them have their churches quietly to themselves; so that they would be content to let us have ours quietly to ourselves." After that I had told him many considerations, why he had no cause to say so, "Well, well," said he, "I pray God (son Roper) some of us live not till that day," showing me no reason why I should put any doubt therein. To whom I said, "By my troth, Sir, it is very desperately spoken," that vile term (I cry God mercy) did I give him, who by these words perceiving me in a fume, said merrily unto me, "Well, son Roper, it shall not be so, it shall not be so." Whom in sixteen years and more, being in his house conversant with him, I could never perceive him so much as once to fume.

But now to return again where I left: After supplying of imperfections of the dispensation sent (as before is rehearsed) to the Commissioners into England, the King taking the matter for ended, and then meaning no further to proceed in that matter, assigned the Bishop of Durham, and Sir Thomas More to go ambassadors to Cambray, a place neither Imperial nor French, to treat a peace between the French King, the Emperor, and him, in the concluding whereof Sir Thomas More so worthily handled himself (procuring in our league far more benefits unto his realm, than at that time by the King and Council was possible to be compassed), that for his good service in that voyage, the King, when he after made him Lord Chancellor, caused the Duke of Norfolk openly to declare unto the people (as you shall hear hereafter more at large) how much all England was bound unto him.

ow, upon the coming home of the Bishop of Durham and Sir Thomas More from Cambray, the King was as earnest in persuading Sir Thomas More to agree unto the matter of his marriage as before, by many and divers ways provoking him thereunto. For which cause (as it was thought) he the rather soon after made him Lord Chancellor, and further declared unto him, that though at his going over the sea to Cambray, he was in utter despair thereof, yet he had conceived since some good hope to compass it. For albeit his marriage, being against the positive law of the Church, and the written law of God, was holden by the dispensation, yet was there another thing found out of late, he said, whereby his marriage appeared to be so directly against the laws of nature, that it could in no wise by the Church be dispensable, as Dr. Stoksely (whom he had then newly preferred to be Bishop of London, and in that case chiefly credited) was able to instruct him, with whom he prayed him in that point to confer.

FAMILIA THOMÆ MORI ANGL. CANCELL.

THE MORE FAMILY GROUP, 1527

But for all his conference with him, he saw nothing of such force, as could induce him to change his opinion therein; which notwithstanding the bishop showed himself in his report of him to the King's highness so good and favourable, that he said, he found him in his Grace's cause very toward, and desirous to find some good matter wherewith he might truly serve his Grace to his contentation. This Bishop Stoksely being by the Cardinal not long before in the Star Chamber openly put to rebuke, and awarded to the Fleet, not brooking his contumelious usage, and thinking, that forasmuch as the Cardinal, for lack of such forwardness in setting first the King's divorce as his Grace looked for, was out of his Highness' favour, he had now a good occasion offered him to revenge his quarrel against him—further to incense the King's displeasure towards him, busily travailed to invent some colourable device for the King's furtherance in that behalf. Which (as before is mentioned) he to his Grace revealed, hoping thereby to bring the King to the better liking of himself, and the more misliking of the Cardinal. His Highness therefore was soon after of his office displaced, and to Sir Thomas More (the rather to move him to incline to his side) the same in his stead committed. Who between Dukes of Norfolk and Suffolk being brought through Westminster Hall to his place in the Chancery, the Duke of Norfolk, in audience of all the people there assembled, showed, that he was from the King himself straightly charged by special commission there openly, in the presence of all, to make declaration, how much all England was beholden to Sir Thomas More for his good service, and how worthy he was to have the highest room in the Realm, and how dearly his Grace loved and trusted him; for which, said the Duke, he had great cause to rejoice.

Whereunto Sir Thomas More, among many other his humble and wise sayings (not now in my memory) answered, "That although he had good cause to rejoice of his Highness' singular favour towards him, that he had far

above his deserts so highly commended him, yet nevertheless he must for his own part needs confess, that in all things by his Grace alleged he had done no more than was his duty. And further disabled himself as unmeet for that room, wherein, considering how wise and honourable a prelate had lately before taken so great a fall, he had," he said, "thereof no cause to rejoice." And as they on the King's behalf charged him uprightly to minister indifferent justice to the people without corruption or affection, so did he likewise charge them again, that if they saw him at any time in anything digress from any part of his duty, in that honourable office, then, as they would discharge their own duty and fidelity to God and the King, so should they not fail to disclose it to his Grace, who otherwise might have just occasion to lay his fault wholly to their charge. While he was Lord Chancellor (being at leisure, as seldom he was) one of his sons-in-law on a time said merrily unto him, "When Cardinal Wolsey was Lord Chancellor, not only divers of his privy chamber, but such also as were his door keepers got great gain, and since he had married one of his daughters, and gave still attendance upon him, he thought he might of reason look for somewhat, where he indeed, because he was ready himself to hear every man, poor and rich, and keep no doors shut from them, could find none, which was to him a great discouragement. And whereas else some for friendship, some for kindred, and some for profit, would gladly have his furtherance in bringing them to his presence, if he should now take anything of them he knew" (he said), "he should do them great wrong, for that they might do as much for themselves, as he could do for them: which condition although he thought in Sir Thomas More very commendable, yet to him" (said he) "being his son he found it nothing profitable." When he had told him this tale, "You say well, son" (quoth he), "I do not mislike that you are of conscience so scrupulous, but many other ways be there (son), that I may do both yourself good, and pleasure your friend also. For sometimes may I in words stand your friend in stead, and sometime may I by my letter help you and him, or if he have a cause depending before me, at your request I may hear him before another, or if his cause be not all the best, yet may I move the parties to fall to some reasonable end by arbitrament; howbeit, this one thing I assure thee on my faith, that if the parties will at my hand call for justice, then were it my father stood on the one side and the devil on the other side (his cause being good) the devil should have right." So offered he his son as he thought (he said) as much favour as with reason he could require.

And that he would for no respect digress from justice well appeared by a plain example of another of his sons-in-law, Mr. Heron. For when he, having a matter before him in the Chancery, presuming too much of his favour, would by him in no wise be persuaded to agree to any indifferent order, then made he in conclusion a flat decree against him. This Lord Chancellor used commonly every af-

ternoon to sit in his open hall, to the
intent, if any person had any suit unto him, they might the more boldly
come to his presence, and there open
complaints before him. Whose manner was also to read every bill himself, ere he would award any subpœna, which bearing matter sufficient worthy a subpœna, would he
set his hand unto, or else cancel it.
Whensoever he passed through Westminster Hall to his place in the Chancery by the Court of the King's
Bench, if his father, one of the judges
there, had been sat ere he came he
would go into the same court, and
there reverently kneeling down in the
sight of them all duly ask his father's
blessing. And if it fortuned that his
father and he at readings in Lincoln's
Inn met together (as they sometime
did) notwithstanding his high office
he would offer in argument the pre-
eminence to his father, though he for
his office sake would refuse to take it.
And for the better declaration of his
natural affection towards his father,
he not only (when he lay on his
death-bed) according to his duty oft-
times with comfortable words most

kindly came to visit him; but also at his departure out of this world, with tears taking him about the neck, most lovingly kissed and embraced him, commending into the merciful hands of Almighty God, and so departed from him. And as few injunctions as he granted while he was Lord Chancellor, yet were they by some of the judges of the law misliked, which I understanding, declared the same unto Sir Thomas More, who answered me, that they have little cause to find fault with him therefore. And thereupon caused he one Mr. Crooke, chief of the six clerks, to make a docket, containing the whole number and causes of all such injunctions, as either in his time had already passed, or at that present time depended in any of the King's Courts at Westminster before him. Which done he invited all the judges to dinner with him in the Council Chamber at Westminster, where after dinner when he had broken with them what complaints he had heard of his injunctions, and moreover showed them both the number and causes of every of them in order so plainly, that, upon full debating of those matters, they were all enforced to confess, that they, in like case, could have done no otherwise themselves, then offered he this unto them, that if the justices of every court, unto whom the reformation of rigour of the law, by reason of their office, most specially appertained, would, upon reasonable considerations, by their own discretions (as they were, as he thought, in conscience bound) mitigate and reform the rigour of the law themselves, there should from thenceforth by him no more injunctions be granted. Whereupon when they refused to condescend, then said he unto them: "Forasmuch as yourselves, my lords, drive me to that necessity for awarding our injunctions to relieve the people's injury, you cannot hereafter any more justly blame me;" after that he had said secretly unto me: "I perceive, son, why they like not so to do. For they see, that they may, by the verdict of the jury, cast off all quarrels from themselves upon them, which they account their chief defence, and therefore am I compelled to abide the ad-

venture of all such reports."

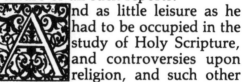nd as little leisure as he had to be occupied in the study of Holy Scripture, and controversies upon religion, and such other like virtuous exercises, being in manner continually busied about the affairs of the King and the Realm, yet such watch and pain in setting forth of divers profitable works in defence of the true Catholic religion against heresies, secretly sown abroad in the Realm, assuredly sustained he, that the bishops, to whose pastoral cure the reformation thereof principally appertained, thinking themselves by his travail (wherein, by their own confession, with him they were not able to make comparison) of their duty discharged, and considering that, for all his pains, and prince's favour, he was no rich man, nor in yearly revenues advanced as his worthiness deserved, therefore at a convocation among themselves and other of the clergy, they agreed together, and concluded upon a sum of four or five thousand pounds at the least (to my remembrance) for his

pains to recompense him. To the payment whereof every bishop, abbot, and the rest of the clergy were after the rate of their abilities liberal contributaries, hoping this portion should be to his contentation. Whereupon Tunstall bishop of Durham, Clarke bishop of Bath, and (as far as I can call to mind) Vaysie bishop of Exeter, repaired unto him, declaring how thankfully for his travails to their discharge in God's cause bestowed, they reckoned themselves bound to consider him. And that albeit they could not according to his deserts so worthily as they gladly would requite him therefore, but reserve that only to the goodness of God, yet for a small part of recompense, in respect of his estate, so unequal to his worthiness, in the name of their whole Convocation, they presented unto him that sum, which they desired him to take in good part, who forsaking it, said, "That like as it were no small comfort unto him, that so wise and learned men so well accepted his simple doing, for which he intended never to receive reward but at the hands of God only, to whom alone was thanks thereof chiefly to be ascribed: so gave he most humble thanks unto their honours all for their bountiful consideration." When they for all their importune pressing upon him, that few would have believed he could have refused it, could by no means make him to take it, then they besought him be content, yet that they might bestow it upon his wife and children; "Not so, my Lords" (quoth he), "I had liever see it all cast into the Thames, than I, or any of mine should have thereof the worth of one penny. For though your offer, my Lords, be indeed very friendly and honourable, yet set I so much by my pleasure, and so little by my profit, that I would not (in good faith) for so much, and much more to have lost the rest of so many a night's sleep, as was spent upon the same. And yet wish I would, for all that, upon conditions that all heresies were suppressed, that all my books were burned, and my labour utterly lost." Thus departing, were they fain to restore to every man his own again.

JOHN FISHER, Bishop of Rochester

This Lord Chancellor albeit he was to God and the world well known of notable virtue, though not so of every man considered, yet for the avoidance of singularity would he appear no otherwise than other men in his apparel and other outward behaviour. And albeit he appeared honourable outwardly, and like one of his calling, yet inwardly he no such vanities esteeming, secretly next his body wore a shirt of hair, which my sister More, a young gentlewoman in the summer, as he sat at supper singly in his doublet and hose, wearing thereupon a plain shirt without ruff or collar, chancing to espy, began to laugh at it. My wife not ignorant of his manner, perceiving the same privily told him of it, and he being sorry that she saw it, presently amended it. He used also sometimes to punish his body with whips, the cords knotted, which was known only to my wife his eldest daughter, whom for her secrecy above all other he specially trusted, caused her, as need required, to wash the same shirt of hair.

ow shortly upon his entry into the high office of the Chancellorship, the King oftsoons again moved him to weigh and consider his greatest matter, who falling down upon his knees, humbly besought his Highness to stand his gracious Sovereign, as ever since his entry into his gracious service he had found him, saying, "There was nothing in the world had been so grievous to his heart as to remember he was not able, as he willingly would with the loss of one of his limbs, for that matter to find anything whereby he could serve his Grace's contentment, as he that always bare in mind the most godly words, that his Highness spake unto him at his first coming into his noble service, the most virtuous lesson that ever prince taught his servant, willing him first to look unto God, and after God to him, as in good faith," he said, "he did, or else might his Grace well account him his most unworthy servant." To this the King answered, "that if he could not with his conscience serve him, he was content to accept his service other-

wise, and use the advice of other his
learned Council, whose consciences
could well enough agree thereto, he
would nevertheless continue his gracious favour towards him, and never
with that matter molest his conscience after." But Sir Thomas More
in process of time seeing the King
fully determined to proceed forth in
the marriage of Queen Anne, and
when he with the bishops and nobles
of the Higher House of Parliament,
were, for the furtherance of that marriage, commanded by the King to go
down to the Common House to show
to them both what the Universities as
well of other parts beyond the seas,
as at Oxford and Cambridge had
done in that behalf, and their seals
also testifying the same: all which
matters, at the King's request (not
showing of what mind himself was
therein), he opened to the Lower
House of the Parliament: nevertheless doubting lest further attempts
should after follow, which, contrary
to his conscience, by reason of his office he was likely to be put unto, he
made suit to the Duke of Norfolk, his
singular dear friend, to be a mean to

the King, that he might, with his Grace's favour, be discharged of that chargeable room of Chancellorship, wherein for certain infirmities of his body, he pretended himself unable any longer to serve. This Duke coming on a time to Chelsea to dine with him, fortuned to find him at church singing in the choir with a surplice on his back; to whom after service, as they went home together arm in arm, the Duke said, "God body, God body (my Lord Chancellor) a parish clerk, a parish clerk, you dishonour the King and his office." "Nay," quoth Sir Thomas More, smiling upon the Duke, "your Grace may not think, that the King, your master and mine, will with me for serving God his Master be offended, or thereby count his office dishonoured." When the Duke, being thereunto solicited by importunate suit, had at length obtained for Sir Thomas More a clear discharge of his office, then at a time convenient, by his Highness' appointment, repaired he to his Grace, to yield up unto him the great seal, which, as his Grace with thanks and praise for his worthy service in that

office courteously at his hands received, so pleased it his Highness to say more unto him, that for the good service he before had done him in any suit which he should after have unto him, that either should concern his honour (for that word it liked his Highness to use unto him) or that should appertain unto his profit, he would find his Highness a good and gracious lord unto him.

After he had thus given over his Chancellorship, and placed all his gentlemen and yeomen with bishops and noblemen, and his eight watermen with the Lord Audley, that after in the same office succeeded him, to whom also he gave his great barge, then calling us that were his children unto him, and asking our advice, how we might now, in this decay of his ability, by the surrender of his office so impaired, that he could not, as he was wont, and gladly would bear out the whole charges of them all himself, from henceforth be able to live and continue together, as he wished we should; when he saw us all silent, and in that case not ready to show our opinions unto him, "Then will I" (said he) "show my poor mind unto you. I have been brought up at Oxford, at an Inn of Chancery, at Lincoln's Inn, and in the King's Court, so forth from the lowest degree to the highest, and yet have I in yearly revenues little more than one hundred pounds by the year at this present left me. So that we must needs hereafter, if we like to live together, be contented to become contributors together. But by my counsel it shall not be best for us to fall to the lowest fare first. We will not therefore descend to Oxford fare, nor to the fare of New Inn, but we will begin with Lincoln's Inn diet, where many right worshipful and of good years do live full well, which if we find not ourselves the first year able to maintain, then will we the next year after go one step down to New Inn fare, wherewith many an honest man is well contented. If that exceed our ability too, then will we the next year after descend to Oxford fare, where many grave, ancient, and learned Fathers be conversant continually, which if our ability stretch not to maintain neither, then may we yet with bags and wallets go a-begging together, and hoping that for pity some good folks will give their charity at every man's door to sing *salve Regina*, and so still keep company merrily together."

And whereas you have heard before he was by the King from a very worshipful living taken unto his Grace's service, with whom all the great and weighty causes that concerned his Highness, of the Realm, he consumed and spent with painful cares, travail, and trouble as well beyond the seas, as within the Realm, in effect the whole substance of his life, yet with all the gain he got thereby (being never no wasteful spender thereof) was he not able, after the resignation of his office of the Lord Chancellor, for the maintenance of himself, and such as necessarily belonged unto him, sufficiently to find meat, drink, fuel, apparel, and such other necessary charges. All the land that ever he purchased before he was Lord Chancellor, was not, I am well assured, above the value of twenty marks by the year,

and after his debts paid he had not I
know (his chain excepted) in gold
and silver left him the worth of one
hundred pounds. And whereas upon
the holidays, during High Chancellorship, one of his gentlemen, when
service at the church was down, ordinarily used to come to my Lady, his
wife's pew and say, "Madam, my
Lord is gone," the next holiday after
the surrender of his office, and departure of his gentlemen he came unto
my Lady, his wife's pew, himself,
and making a low curtsey, said unto
her, "Madam, my Lord is gone." In
the time somewhat before his trouble, he would talk with his wife and
children of the joys of heaven and the
pains of hell, of the lives of holy mar-
tyrs, and of their grievous martyr-
dom, of their marvellous patience,
and of their passions and deaths, that
they suffered rather than they would
offend God, and what an happy and
a blessed thing it was for the love of
God to suffer loss of goods, imprisonment, loss of lands, and life also.
He would further say unto them, that
upon his faith if he might perceive his
wife and children would encourage

him to die in a good cause, it should so comfort him, that for very joy thereof it would make him merrily to run to death. He showed them afore what trouble might fall unto him wherewith, and the like virtuous talk he had so long before his trouble encouraged them, that when he after fell in the trouble indeed, his trouble to him was a great deal the less, *quia spicula prævisa minus lædunt.*

ow upon this resignment of his office came Sir Thomas Cromwell (then in the King's high favour) to Chelsea to him on a message from the King, wherein when they had throughly communed together, "Mr. Cromwell" (quoth he), "you are now entered into the service of a most noble, wise, and liberal prince; if you will follow my poor advice you shall, in counsel giving unto his Grace, ever tell him what he ought to do, but never tell him what he is able to do, so shall you show yourself a true faithful servant, and a right worthy Councillor. For if the lion knew his own strength, hard were it for any man to rule him."

Shortly thereupon was there a commission directed to Cranmer, then Archbishop of Canterbury to determine the matter of the matrimony between the King and Queen Katherine at St. Alban's, where according to the King's mind that was throughly finished, who pretending that he had no justice at the Pope's hands, from thenceforth sequestered himself from the See of Rome, and so married the Lady Anne Bullen, which Sir Thomas More understanding, said unto me, "God give grace, son, that these matters within a while be not confirmed with oaths." I at that time seeing no likelihood thereof, yet fearing lest for his forespeaking that would the sooner come to pass, waxed therefore for his saying much offended with him. It fortuned not long before the coming of the Queen Anne through the streets of London from the Tower to Westminster to her Coronation, that he received a letter from the Bishops of Durham, Bath, and Winchester, requesting him to bear them com-

pany from the Tower to the Coronation and also to take £20 that by the bearer thereof they had sent him to buy a gown with, which he thankfully received, and at home still tarrying, at their next meeting said merrily unto them, "My Lords, in the letters which you lately sent me, you required two things of me, the one whereof since I was so well contented to grant you, the other therefore I thought I might be the bolder to deny you."

In continuance when the King saw that he could by no manner of benefits win him to his side, then went he about by terrors and threats to drive him thereunto, the beginning of which trouble grew by occasion of a certain nun dwelling in Canterbury, for her virtue and holiness among the people not a little esteemed, unto whom for that cause many religious persons, Doctors of Divinity, and divers other of good worship of the laity used to resort, who affirming that she had revelations from God to give the King warning of his wicked life, and of the

MARGARET GIGS (MRS. CLEMENT) in her 22nd year

abuses of the sword and authority committed to him by God, and understanding my Lord of Rochester, Bishop Fisher, to be a man of notable virtuous living and learning, repaired to Rochester, and there disclosed unto him all her revelations, desiring his advice and counsel therein, which the Bishop perceiving might well stand with the laws of God and his Church advised her (as she before had warning and intended) to go to the King herself, and to let him understand the whole circumstance thereof, whereupon she went unto the King, and told him all her revelations, and returned home again. And in short space after, she making a voyage to the Nun of Sion by the means of one Mr. Reynolds a father of that house there fortuned concerning such secrets as she had revealed unto her, some part whereof seemed to touch the matter of the King's supremacy and marriage (which shortly thereupon followed) to enter into talk with Sir Thomas More; who notwithstanding he might well at that time without danger of any law (though after, as himself had prognosticated before, those matters were established by statutes and confirmed by oaths) freely and safely have talked with her therein; nevertheless, in all the communication between them (as in process of time it appeared) had always so discreetly demeaned himself, that he deserved not to be blamed, but contrariwise to be commended and praised. And had he not been one that in all his great office, and doings for the King and Realm together, had from all corruption of wrong doing, or bribes taking, kept himself so clear; that no man was able therewith to blemish him, it would without doubt (in this troublesome time of the King's wrath and indignation towards him) have been deeply laid to his charge, and of the King's Highness favourably accepted, as in the case of one Parnell that most manifestly appeared: against whom Sir Thomas More while he was Lord Chancellor, at the suit of one Vaughan his adversary had made a decree.

his Parnell to the King's
Highness had grievously
complained that Sir
Thomas More, for mak-
ing the decree, had of
the same Vaughan (unable for the
gout to travel abroad himself) by the
hands of his wife taken a fair great
gilt cup for a bribe, who thereupon
by the King's appointment being
called before the Council, where that
matter was heinously laid to his
charge, forthwith confessed, that forasmuch as that cup was long after the
aforesaid decree brought unto him
for a new year's gift, he upon her importunate pressing upon him, therefore of courtesy refused not to take
it. Then the Lord of Wiltshire (for ha-
tred of his religion preferrer of this
suit) with much rejoicing said unto
the Lords, "Lo my Lords, lo, did I not
tell you that you should find this
matter true?" Whereupon Sir
Thomas More desired their worships,
that as they had courteously heard
him tell the one part of his tale, so
they would vouchsafe of their honours indifferently to hear the other,
after which obtained, he further de-

clared unto them, that albeit indeed he had with much work received that cup, yet immediately thereupon he caused his butler to fill that with wine, and of that cup drank to her, and that when she had pledged him, then as freely as her husband had given it unto him, even so freely gave he the same unto her again, to give unto her husband for his new year's gift, which at his instant request, though much against her will, yet at length she was fain to receive, as herself and certain other there presently deposed before them. Thus was the great mountain turned scarce unto a mole-hill.

So I remember that another time on a new year's day there came unto him one Mrs. Crocker, a rich widow (for whom with no small pains he had made a decree in the Chancery against the Lord of Arundel) to present him with a pair of gloves and £40 in angels in them for a new year's gift, of whom he thankfully received the gloves, but refusing the money said unto her, "Mistress, since that were against good manners to forsake a gentlewoman's new year's gift, I am content to receive your gloves, but as for your money I utterly refuse:" so much against her mind enforced he her to take her gold again. And one Mr. Gresham likewise having a cause depending in the Chancery against him, sent him for a new year's gift a fair gilt cup, the fashion whereof he very well liking caused one of his own (though not in his fantasy of so good a fashion) yet better in value, to be brought out of his chamber, which he willed the messenger to deliver to his mistress in recompense, and under other conditions would he in no wise receive it. Many things more of like effect for the declaration of his innocence and clearness from corruption, or evil affection, could I here rehearse besides, which for tediousness omitting, I refer to the readers by these few fore-remembered examples with their own judgments wisely to consider.

t this Parliament was there put into the Lords' House a bill to attaint the nun, and divers other religious persons of high treason; and the Bishop of Rochester, Sir Thomas More, and certain others of misprision of treason: the King presupposing of likelihood this bill would be to Sir Thomas More so troublous and terrible, that that would force him to relent and condescend to his request, wherein his Grace was much deceived. To which bill Sir Thomas More was a suitor personally to be received in his own defence to make answer, but the King not liking that, assigned the Archbishop of Canterbury, the Lord Chancellor, the Duke of Norfolk, and Mr. Cromwell, at a day and place appointed to call Sir Thomas More before them, at which time I thinking I had good opportunity, earnestly advised him to labour unto these Lords for the help of his discharge out of the Parliament Bill; who answered me, he would: and at his coming before them according to their appointment, they entertained

79

him very friendly, willing him to sit down with them, which in no wise he would. Then began the Lord Chancellor to declare unto him how many ways the King had showed his love and favour toward him, how fain he would have had him continue in his office, how glad he would have been to have heaped more benefits upon him, and finally, how he could ask no worldly honour, or profit at his Highness' hands, that were likely to be denied him; hoping by the declaration of the King's kindness and favour towards him to provoke him to recompense his Grace with the like again, and unto those things that the Parliament, the Bishops, and Universities had already passed to yield his consent. To this Sir Thomas More mildly answered saying, "No man living is there (my Lords) that would with better will do the thing that should be acceptable to the King's Highness than I, which must needs confess his manifold benefits, and bountiful goodness most benignly bestowed on me. Howbeit I verily hoped that I should never have heard of this matter more, considering that

I have from time to time always from the beginning so plainly and truly declared my mind unto his Grace, which his Highness to me ever seemed, like a most gracious prince, very well to accept, never minding, as he said, to molest me more therewith. Since which time any further thing that was able to move me to any change could I never find, and if I could, there is none in all the world that could have been gladder of it than I." Many things more were there of like sort on both sides uttered. But in the end when they saw they could by no means of persuasions remove him from his former determinations, then began they more terribly to touch him, telling him that the King's Highness had given them in commandment (if they could by no gentleness win him) in his name with his great ingratitude to charge him, that never was there servant to his master so villainous, nor subject to his prince so traitorous as he. For he by his subtle sinister sleights, most unnaturally procuring and provoking him to set forth a book of the assertion of Seven Sacraments, and in

maintenance of the Pope's authority, had caused him to his dishonor throughout all Christendom to put a sword in the Pope's hands to fight against himself. When they had thus laid forth all the terrors they could imagine against him: "My Lords" (quoth he) "These terrors be the arguments for children, and not for me. But to answer that wherewith you do chiefly burden me, I believe the King's Highness of his honour will never lay that to my charge. For none is there that in that point can say more in mine excuse than his Highness himself, who right well knoweth that I was never procurer or councillor of his Majesty thereunto but after that it was finished, by his Grace's appointment, and consent of the makers of the same, only a sorter out, and placer of the principal matters therein contained; wherein when I found the Pope's authority highly advanced, and with strong arguments mightily defended, I said unto his Grace, *I must put your Grace in remembrance of one thing, and that is this, The Pope (as your Grace knoweth) is a Prince as you are, and*

*in league with all other Christian
Princes, that may hereafter so fall
out, that your Grace and he may
vary upon some points of the league,
whereupon may grow some breach
of amity and war between you both;
I think it best therefore that that
place be amended, and his authority
more slenderly touched.* Nay (quoth
his Grace) that it shall not, we are so
much bounden unto the See of Rome,
that we cannot do too much honour
unto it. Then did I put him further in
remembrance of the statute of
Praemunire, whereby a good part of
the Pope's pastoral care here was
paid away. To that answered his
Highness, *whatsoever impediment be
to the contrary, we will set forth that
authority to the uttermost. For we received from that See our Crown Imperial;* which till his Grace with his
own mouth told me I never heard of
before. So that I trust when his Grace
shall be truly informed of this, and
call to his gracious remembrance my
doings in that behalf, his Highness
will never speak of it more, but clear
me throughly therein himself." And
thus displeasantly departed they.

hen took Sir Thomas More his boat towards his house àt Chelsea, wherein by the way he was very merry, and for that was I nothing sorry, hoping that he had gotten himself discharged out of the Parliament Bill. When he was come home, then walked we two alone into his garden together, where I desirous to know how he had sped, said, "Sir, I trust all is well, because you are so merry." "That is so, indeed (son Roper) I thank God" (quoth he). "Are you put out of the Parliament Bill then?" said I. "By my troth (son Roper)," quoth he, "I never remembered it." "Never remembered it, Sir?" quoth I. "A case that toucheth yourself so near, and us all for your sake. I am sorry to hear it. For I verily trusted when I saw you so merry, that all had been well." Then said he, "Wilt thou know, son Roper, why I was so merry?" "That would I gladly, Sir,"quoth I. "In good faith I rejoice, son," (quoth he), "that I had given the devil so foul a fall, and that with those Lords I had gone so far, as

DAME ALICE MORE

without great shame, I could never go back again." At which words waxed I very sad. For though himself liked it well, yet liked it me but a little.

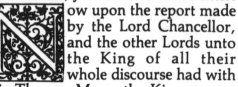ow upon the report made by the Lord Chancellor, and the other Lords unto the King of all their whole discourse had with Sir Thomas More, the King was so highly offended with him, that he plainly told them he was fully determined the said Parliament Bill should undoubtedly proceed forth against him. To whom my Lord Chancellor and the rest of the Lords said, that they perceived the Lords of the Upper House so precisely bent to hear him, in his own case, make answer for himself, that if he were not put out of the Parliament Bill, it would without fail be utterly an overthrow of all. But for all this needs would the King have his own will therein, or else he said that at the passing thereof he would be personally present himself. Then the Lord Audley and the rest, seeing him so vehemently set thereupon, on their knees most humbly besought his Majesty to forbear the

same, considering, that if he should in his own presence receive an overthrow, it would not only encourage his subjects ever after to contemn him, but also throughout all Christendom, redound to his dishonour for ever adding thereunto, that they mistrusted not in time to find some meet matter to serve his Grace's turn better. For in this case of the nun he was accounted so innocent and clear, that for his dealing therein men reckoned him worthier of praise than reproof. Whereupon at length through their earnest persuasion, he was content to condescend to their petition. And on the morrow after, Mr. Cromwell meeting me in the Parliament House willed me to tell my father, that he was put out of the Parliament Bill. But because I had appointed to dine that day in London, I sent the message by my servant to my wife at Chelsea, whereof she informed her father, "in faith Meg" (quoth he) *"Quod defertur, non aufertur."*

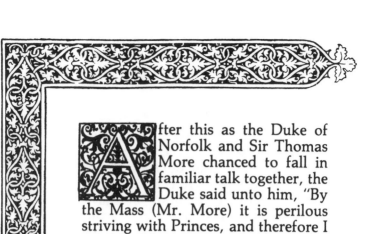

After this as the Duke of Norfolk and Sir Thomas More chanced to fall in familiar talk together, the Duke said unto him, "By the Mass (Mr. More) it is perilous striving with Princes, and therefore I would wish you somewhat to incline to the King's pleasure. For by God's body (Mr. More) *Indignatio principis mors est.*" "Is that all, my Lord?" (quoth he). "Is there (in good faith) no more difference between your Grace and me, but that I shall die to-day and you to-morrow?"

So fell it out within a month or thereabout after the making of the Statute for the oath of Supremacy and Matrimony, that all the priests of London and Westminster, and no temporal men but he were sent to appear at Lambeth before the Bishop of Canterbury, the Lord Chancellor, and Secretary Cromwell, Commissioners, there, to tender the oath unto them. Then Sir Thomas More, as his accustomed manner was always ere he entered into any matter of importance (as when he was first chosen of the King's Privy Council, when he was sent Ambassador, appointed Speaker of the Parliament, made Lord Chancellor, or when he took any like weighty matter upon him) to go to the church, and to be confessed, to hear mass, and be housled; so did he likewise in the morning early the selfsame day that he was summoned to appear before the Lords at Lambeth. And whereas he used evermore before, at his departure from his house and children (whom he loved tenderly) to have them bring him to his boat, and there to kiss them all, and bid them farewell, then would he suffer none of them forth of the gate to follow him, but pulled the wicket after him, and shut them all from him, and with an heavy heart (as by his countenance it appeared) with me, and our four servants, there took his boat towards Lambeth. Wherein sitting still sadly awhile, at the last he rounded me in the ear and said, "Son Roper, I thank our Lord, the field is won." What he meant thereby, then, I wist not. Yet loath to seem ignorant I answered,

"Sir, I am thereof very glad." But as I conjectured afterwards it was for that the love he had to God wrought in him so effectually, that it conquered in him all his carnal affectations utterly.

t his coming to Lambeth, how wisely he behaved himself before the Commissioners, at the ministration of the oath unto him, may be found in certain letters of his (sent to my wife) remaining in a great book of his works: where by the space of four days, he was betaken to the custody of the Abbot of Westminster, during which time the King consulted with his Council what order were meet to be taken with him. And albeit in the beginning they were resolved, that with an oath not to be known whether he had to the supremacy been sworn, or what he thought thereof, he should be discharged, yet did Queen Anne, by her importunate clamour, so sore exasperate the King against him, that, contrary to his former resolution, he caused the oath of the supremacy to be ministered unto him, who, albeit

he made a discreet qualified answer, nevertheless was forthwith committed to the Tower, who as he was going thitherward, wearing, as he commonly did, a chain of gold about his neck, Sir Richard Cromwell (that had the charge of his conveyance thither) advised him to send home his chain to his wife, or some of his children, "Nay, Sir (quoth he), that will I not. For if I were taken in the field by my enemies, I would they should somewhat fare the better by me." At whose landing Mr. Lieutenant at the Tower gate was ready to receive him, where the porter demanded of him his upper garment. "Mr. Porter" (quoth he) "here it is," and took off his cap and delivered him, saying, "I am very sorry it is no better for you." "Nay, Sir" (quoth the Porter), "I must have your gown," and so was he by Mr. Lieutenant conveyed into his lodging, where he called unto him one John a-Wood his own servant there appointed to attend upon him, who could neither write nor read, and swore him before the Lieutenant that if he should hear, or see him at any time, speak or write any manner

of thing against the King, the Council, or the state of the Realm, he should open it to the Lieutenant, that the Lieutenant might incontinent reveal it to the Council.

ow when Sir Thomas More had remained in the Tower a little more than a month, my wife, longing to see her father, by her earnest suit at length gat leave to go to him. At whose coming (after the seven psalms and litany said, which whensoever she came to him, ere he fell in talk of any worldly matters, he used accustomably to say with her) among other communication he said unto her, "I believe (Meg) that they that have put me here, ween they have done me a high displeasure. But I assure you on my faith, mine own dear daughter, if it had not been for my wife and you that be my children, whom I account the chief part of my charge, I would not have failed, long ere this, to have closed myself in as strait a room and straiter too. But since I come hither without mine own desert, I trust that God of his goodness will discharge me of my care, and with his gracious help supply my want among you. I find no cause (I thank God, Meg) to reckon myself in worse case here, than in mine own house. For methinketh God maketh me a wanton, and setteth me on his lap and dandleth me." Thus by his gracious demeanour in tribulations appeared it, that all the troubles that ever chanced unto him by his patient sufferance thereof were to him no painful punishment, but of his patience profitable exercises.

And at another time, when he had first questioned with my wife a while of the order of his wife and children, and state of his house in his absence, he asked her how Queen Anne did: "In faith, father" (quoth she), "never better." "Never better, Meg?" quoth he. "Alas (Meg) alas, it pitieth me to remember, in what misery she (poor soul) shortly shall come." After this Mr. Lieutenant coming into his chamber to visit him, rehearsed the benefits and friendships that he had many times received at his hands, and how much bounden he was therefore friendly to entertain him and make him good cheer, which since (the case standing as it did) he could not do without the King's indignation, he trusted (he said) he would accept his good will, and such poor cheer as he had. "Mr. Lieutenant" (quoth he again), "I verily believe, as you may, so are you my good friends indeed, and would (as you say) with your best cheer entertain me, for the which I most heartily thank you. And assure yourself (Mr. Lieutenant)," quoth he, "I do not mislike my cheer, but whensoever I do so, then thrust me out of your doors."

Whereas the oath confirming the supremacy and matrimony was by the first statute comprised in few words, the Lord Chancellor and Mr. Secretary did of their own heads add more words unto it, to make it appear to the King's ears more pleasant and plausible. And that oath so amplified caused they to be ministered to Sir Thomas More and to all other throughout the Realm, which Sir

Thomas perceiving said unto my wife: "I may tell thee (Meg) they that have committed me hither for refusing of the oath, not agreeable with the statute, are not able by their own law to justify my imprisonment. And surely (daughter) it is a great pity that a Christian prince should (by a flexible council ready to follow his affections, and by a weak clergy lacking grace constantly to stand to their learning) with flattery so shameful to be abused." But at length the Lord Chancellor and Mr. Secretary, espying their oversight in that behalf, were fain afterwards to find the means that another statute should be made for the confirmation of the oath so amplified with their additions.

After Sir Thomas More had given over his office and all other worldly doings therewith, to the intent he might from thenceforth the more quietly set himself to the service of God, then made he a conveyance for the disposition of his lands, reserving for himself an estate thereof only for the term of his

life, and after his decease assuring
some part of the same to his wife,
some to his son's wife for a jointure,
in consideration that she was an in-
heritrix in possession of more than an
hundred pounds land by the year,
and some to me and my wife in recompense of our marriage money
with divers remainders over, all
which conveyance and assurance was
perfectly finished long before that
matter, whereupon she was at-
tainted, was made an offence, and
yet after by statute clearly voided;
and so were all his lands, that he had
to his wife and children by the said
conveyance in such sort assured,
contrary to the order of law, taken
away from them, and brought into
the King's hands, saving that portion
that he had appointed to my wife and
me, which although he had in the
foresaid conveyance reserved, as he
did the rest, for term of his life unto
himself, nevertheless, upon further
consideration after by another conveyance he gave that same immediately to me, and my wife in possession. And so because the statute had
undone only the first conveyance,

ERASMUS

giving no more to the King but so much as passed by that, the second conveyance, whereby it was given unto my wife and me, being dated two days after was without the compass of the statute, and so was our portion to us by that means clearly reserved.

As Sir Thomas More in the Tower chanced on a time looking out of his window to behold one Mr. Reynolds, a religious, learned and virtuous father of Sion, and three monks of the Charterhouse for the matter of the supremacy going out of the Tower to execution, he, as one longing in that journey to have accompanied them, said unto my wife, then standing there beside him, "Lo, dost thou not see (Meg) that these blessed fathers be now as cheerful going to their deaths, as bridegrooms to their marriages? Wherefore thereby mayest thou see (mine own good daughter) what a difference there is between such as have in effect spent all their days in a strait, hard, penitential, and painful life religiously, and such as have in

the world, like worldly wretches, as thy poor father hath done, consumed all the time in pleasure and ease licentiously. For God, considering their long-continued life in most sore and grievous penance, will not longer suffer them to remain here in this vale of misery, and iniquity, but speedily hence take them to the fruition of his everlasting deity: whereas thy silly father (Meg) that, like a most wicked caitiff, hath passed forth the whole course of his miserable life most pitifully, God, thinking him not worthy so soon to come to that eternal felicity, leaveth him here yet, still in the world further to be plunged and turmoiled with misery."

Within a while after Mr. Secretary (coming to him into the Tower from the King) pretended much friendship towards him, and for his comfort told him, that the King's Highness was his good and gracious lord and minded not with any matter, wherein he should have any cause of scruple, from henceforth to trouble his conscience. As soon as Mr. Secretary was gone, to

express what comfort he conceived of his words, he wrote with a coal (for ink then he had none) these verses following:—

> "Ay flattering fortune
>   look you never so fair,
> Nor never so pleasantly
>   begin to smile,
> As though thou wouldst
>   my ruins all repair
> During my life thou
>   shalt not me beguile,
> Trust I shall, God, to
>   enter in a while
> Thy haven of heaven
>   sure and uniform,
> Ever after thy calm look
>   I for no storm."

When Sir Thomas More had continued a good while in the Tower, my lady his wife obtained licence to see him, who at her first coming like a simple woman, and somewhat worldly too, with this manner of salutations bluntly saluted him, "What the good year, Mr. More," quoth she, "I marvel that you, that have been always hitherunto taken for so wise a man, will now so play the fool to lie here in this close filthy prison, and be content to be shut up among mice and rats, when you might be abroad at your liberty, and with the favour and good will both of the King and his Council, if you would but do as all the bishops and best learned of this Realm have done. And seeing you have at Chelsea a right fair house, your library, your books, your gallery, your garden, your orchards, and all other necessaries so handsomely about you, where you might, in the company of me your wife, your children, and household be merry, I muse what a God's name you mean here still thus fondly to tarry." After he had a while quietly heard her, with a cheerful countenance he said unto her, "I pray thee good Mrs. Alice, tell me, tell me one thing." "What is that?" (quoth she). "Is not this house as nigh heaven as mine own?" To whom she, after her accustomed fashion, not liking such talk, answered, *"Tille valle, tille valle."* "How say you, Mrs. Alice, is it not so?" He quoth. *"Bone Deus, bone Deus,* man, will this gear never be left?" quoth she. "Well then, Mrs. Alice, if it be so, it is very well. For I see no great cause why I should much joy of my gay house, or of anything belonging thereunto, when, if I should but seven years lie buried under the ground, and then arise and come thither again, I should not fail to find some therein that would bid me get me out of the doors, and tell me that were none of mine. What cause have I then to like such an house as would so soon forget his master?" So her persuasions moved him but a little.

ot long after came there to him the Lord Chancellor, the Dukes of Norfolk and Suffolk, with Mr. Secretary, and certain others of the Privy Council at two separate times, by all policies possible procuring him either precisely to confess the supremacy, or precisely to deny it. Whereunto (as appeareth by his examination in the said great book) they could never bring him. Shortly hereupon Mr. Rich (afterwards Lord Rich) then newly the King's Solicitor, Sir Richard South-

well, and Mr. Palmer, servant to the Secretary, were sent to Sir Thomas More into the Tower, to fetch away his books from him. And while Sir Richard Southwell and Mr. Palmer were busy in trussing up of his books, Mr. Rich pretending friendly talk with him, among other things of a set course, as it seemed, said thus unto him: "Forasmuch as it is well known (Mr. More) that you are a man both wise and well learned, as well in the laws of the Realm, as otherwise, I pray you therefore, Sir, let me be so bold as of good will to put unto you this case. Admit there were, Sir," quoth he, "an Act of Parliament, that all the Realm should take me for the King, would not you (Mr. More) take me for the King?" "Yes, Sir," quoth Sir Thomas More, "that would I." "I put the case further" (quoth Mr. Rich) "that there were an Act of Parliament that all the Realm should take me for the Pope; would then not you, Mr. More, take me for the Pope?" "For answer," quoth Sir Thomas More, "to your first case, the Parliament may well (Mr. Rich) meddle with the state of temporal princes; but to make answer to your second case, I will put you this case. Suppose the Parliament would make a law, that God should not be God, would you then, Mr. Rich, say God were not God?" "No, Sir," quoth he, "that would I not, since no Parliament may make any such law." "No more" (said Sir Thomas More, as Mr. Rich reported of him) "could the Parliament make the King supreme head of the Church." Upon whose only report was Sir Thomas More indicted of treason upon the Statute in which it was made treason to deny the King to be supreme head of the Church, into which indictment were put these words, *maliciously, traitorously, and diabolically.*

hen Sir Thomas More was brought from the Tower to Westminster Hall to answer the indictment, and at the King's Bench bar before the judges thereupon arraigned, he openly told them that he would upon that indictment have abiden in law, but he thereby should have been driven to confess of

himself the matter indeed, which was the denial of the King's supremacy, which he protested was untrue, wherefore thereto he pleaded not guilty, and so reserved unto himself advantage to be taken of the body of the matter after verdict, to avoid that indictment. And moreover added, "if those only odious terms, *maliciously, traitorously, and diabolically* were put out of the indictment, he saw nothing therein justly to charge him." And for proof to the jury that Sir Thomas More was guilty to this treason, Mr. Rich was called by them to give evidence unto them, as he did; against whom Sir Thomas More began in this wise to say: "If I were a man (my Lords) that did not regard an oath, I need not (as it is well known) in this place, at this time, nor in this case to stand as an accused person. And if this oath of yours (Mr. Rich) be true, then pray I that I may never see God in the face, which I would not say, were it otherwise, to win the whole world." Then recited he unto the discourse of all their communication in the Tower according to the truth, and said, "In faith, Mr.

Rich, I am sorrier for your perjury
than for mine own peril, and you
shall understand that neither I, nor
no man else to my knowledge ever
took you to be a man of such credit
as in any matter of importance I, or
any other would at any time vouchsafe to communicate with you. And
(as you know) of no small while I
have been acquainted with you and
your conversation, who have known
you from your youth hitherto. For
we long dwelled both in one parish
together, where, as yourself can tell
(I am sorry you compel me so to say)
you were esteemed very light of your
tongue, a great dicer, and of not
commendable fame. And so in your
house at the Temple (where hath been
your chief bringing up) were you
likewise accounted. Can it therefore
seem likely unto your honourable
Lordships, that I would, in so
weighty a cause, so far overshoot
myself, as to trust Mr. Rich (a man of
me always reputed for one of so little
truth, as your Lordships have heard)
so far above my soverign Lord the
King, or any of his noble councillors,
that I would unto him utter the se-

crets of my conscience touching the King's supremacy, the special point and only mark at my hands so long sought for? A thing which I never did, nor never would, after the Statute thereof made, reveal it, either to the King's Highness himself, or to any of his honourable councillors, as it is not unknown unto your house, at sundry times, and several, sent from his Grace's own person unto the Tower to me for none other purpose. Can this in your judgments (my Lords) seem likely to be true? And if I had so done indeed, my Lords, as Mr. Rich hath sworn, seeing it was spoke but in familiar secret talk, nothing affirming, and only in putting of cases, without other displeasant circumstances, it cannot justly be taken to be spoken maliciously. And where there is no malice there can be no offence. And over this I can never think (my Lords) that so many worthy bishops, so many honourable personages, and many other worshipful, virtuous, wise, and well-learned men, as at the making of that law were in the Parliament as-sembled, ever meant to have any man punished by death, in whom there could be found no malice, taking *malitia pro malevolentia*. For if *malitia* be generally taken for sin, no man is there then that can thereof excuse himself. *Quia si dixerimus quod peccatum non habemus, nosmetipsos seducimus, et veritas in nobis non est.* And only this word *maliciously* is in the Statute material, as this term *forcible* is in the statute of forcible entries; by which statute if a man enter peaceably, and put not his adversary out forcibly, it is no offence, but if he put him out forcibly, then by that statute it is an offence. And so shall he be punished by this term *forcible*. Besides this, the manifold goodness of my sovereign Lord the King's Highness himself that hath been so many ways my singular good Lord and Gracious Sovereign, that hath so dearly loved me, and trusted me even at my first coming into his noble service with the dignity of his honourable Privy Council, vouchsafing to admit me to offices of great credit, and worship most liberally advanced me, and finally with that weighty room of his Grace's high

KING HENRY VIII

Chancellorship (the like whereof he never did to temporal men before) next to his own royal person the highest officer in this noble realm, so far above my merits or qualities able and meet therefore, of his incomparable benignity honoured and exalted me by the space of twenty years and more, showing his continual favour towards me; and (until, at mine own poor suit, it pleased his Highness, giving me licence, with his Majesty's favour, to bestow the residue of my life wholly for the provision of my soul in the service of God, of his special goodness thereof to discharge and unburden me) most benignly heaped honours more and more upon me; all this his Highness' goodness, I say, so long continued towards me, were, in my mind (my Lords), matter sufficient to convince this slanderous surmise (by this man) so wrongfully imagined against me." Mr. Rich seeing himself so disproved, and his credit so foully defaced, caused Sir Richard Southwell and Mr. Palmer, that at that time of their communication were in the chamber, to be sworn what words had passed betwixt them. Whereupon Mr. Palmer on his deposition said, that he was so busy about the trussing up Sir Thomas More's books in a sack, that he took no heed to their talk. Sir Richard Southwell likewise upon his deposition said, that because he was appointed only to look to the conveyance of his books, he gave no ear unto them. After this, were there many other reasons (not now in my remembrance) by Sir Thomas More in his own defence alleged, to the discredit of Mr. Rich his foresaid evidence, and proof of the clearness of his own conscience. All which notwithstanding the jury found him guilty, and incontinent upon the verdict the Lord Chancellor (for that matter chief commissioner) beginning in judgment against him, Sir Thomas More said to him, "My Lord, when I was towards the law, the manner in such case was to ask the prisoner before judgment, why judgment should not be given against him?" Whereupon the Lord Chancellor staying his judgement, wherein he had partly proceeded, demanded of him what he was able to say to the contrary? Who then in this sort mildly made answer: "Forasmuch as, my Lord" (quoth he), "this indictment is grounded upon an Act of Parliament, directly oppugnant to the laws of God and his holy Church, the supreme government of which, or of any part thereof, may no temporal prince presume by any law to take upon him as rightfully belonging to the See of Rome, a spiritual pre-eminence by the mouth of our Saviour himself, personally present upon the earth, to St. Peter and his successors, bishops of the same see, by special prerogative, granted, it is therefore in law amongst Christian men insufficient to charge any Christian." And for proof thereof like as amongst divers other reasons and authorities he declared That this Realm, being but one member and small part of the Church, might not make a particular law dischargeable with the general law of Christ's holy Catholic Church, no more than the City of London, being but one poor member in respect of the whole Realm, might make a law against an Act of Parliament to bind the whole Realm unto; so further showed he, that it was contrary both to the laws and statutes of this land, yet unrepealed, as they might evidently perceive in *Magna charta*, *Quod Ecclesia Anglicana libera sit et habeat omnia jura sua integra, et libertates suas illæsas*, and contrary to that sacred oath which the King's Highness himself, and every other Christian prince always at their coronations received, alleging moreover, that no more might this Realm of England refuse obedience to the See of Rome, than might the child refuse obedience to his natural father. For as St. Paul said of the Corinthians, "I have regenerated you my children in Christ," so might St. Gregory Pope of Rome (of whom by St. Augustine his messenger we first received the Christian faith) of us English men truly say, "You are my children, because I have given to you everlasting salvation, a far better inheritance than any carnal father can leave unto his child, and by spiritual generation have made you my spiritual children in Christ." Then was it thereunto by the Lord Chancellor answered, that seeing all the bishops, universities,

and best learned men of the Realm
had to this Act agreed, it was much
marvelled that he alone against them
all would so stiffly stick and vehe-
mently argue there against. To that
Sir Thomas More replied saying, "If
the number of bishops and universities be so material, as your Lordships
seemeth to take it, then see I little
cause (my Lords) why that thing in
my conscience should make any
change. For I nothing doubt, but that
though not in this Realm, yet in
Christendom about they be not the
least part, that be of my mind
therein. But if I should speak of those
that be already dead (of whom many
be now saints in heaven) I am very
sure it is the far greater part of them,
that all the while they lived, thought
in this case that way that I think
now. And therefore am I not bound
(my Lords) to conform my conscience to the council of one realm
against the General Council of Christendom." Now when Sir Thomas
More, for the avoiding of the indictment, had taken as many exceptions
as he thought meet and more reasons
than I can now remember alleged, the

Lord Chancellor, loath to have the burden of the judgment wholly to depend upon himself, then openly asked the advice of the Lord Fitz-James, then the Lord Chief Justice of the King's Bench, and joined in commission with him, whether this indictment were sufficient or not? Who like a wise man answered, "My Lords all, by St. Julian" (that was ever his oath) "I must needs confess, that if the Act of Parliament be not unlawful, then is not the indictment in my conscience insufficient." Whereupon the Lord Chancellor said to the rest of the Lords, "Lo, my Lords, lo, you hear what my Lord Chief Justice saith," and so immediately gave the judgment against him. After which ended, the commissioners yet courteously offered him, if he had anything else to allege for his defence to grant him favourable audience, who answered, "More have I not to say (my Lords) but like as the blessed Apostle St. Paul, as we read in the Acts of the Apostles, was present, and consented to the death of St. Stephen, and kept their clothes that stoned him to death, and yet be they now both

twain holy saints in heaven, and shall
continue there friends for ever, so I
verily trust and shall therefore right
heartily pray, that though your Lordships have now in earth been judges
to my condemnation, we may yet
hereafter in heaven merrily all meet
together to our everlasting salvation." Thus much touching Sir
Thomas More's arraignment, being
not thereat present myself, have I by
the credible report of Sir Anthony
Sumtleger Knight, and partly of Sir
Richard Heywood, and John Webb
Gentleman, with others of good
credit, at the hearing thereof present
themselves, as far forth as my poor
wit and memory would serve me,
here truly rehearsed unto you.

ow after this arraignment
departed he from the bar
to the Tower again, led
by Sir William Kingston,
a tall, strong, and comely
knight, Constable of the Tower, his
very dear friend, who, when he had
brought him from Westminster to the
Old Swan towards the Tower, there
with a heavy heart, the tears running
down his cheeks, bade him farewell.

Sir Thomas More seeing him so sorrowful, comforted him with as good words as he could, saying, "Good Mr. Kingston, trouble not yourself, but be of good cheer. For I will pray for you, and my good Lady your wife, that we may meet in heaven together, where we shall be merry for ever and ever." Soon after Sir William Kingston talking with me of Sir Thomas More, said, "In faith Mr. Roper I was ashamed of myself, that at my departure from your father, I found my heart so feeble, and his so strong, that he was fain to comfort me which should rather have comforted him."

When Sir Thomas More came from Westminster to the Towerward again his daughter my wife, desirous to see her father, whom she thought she should never see in this world after, and also to have his final blessing, gave attendance about the Tower wharf, where she knew he should pass by, ere he could enter into the Tower. There tarrying for his coming home, as soon as she saw him, after his blessings on her knees reverently received, she, hasting towards, without consideration of care of herself, pressing in amongst the midst of the throng and the Company of the Guard, that with halbards and bills were round about him, hastily ran to him, and there openly in the sight of all them embraced and took him about the neck and kissed him, who well liking her most daughterly love and affection towards him, gave her his fatherly blessing, and many godly words of comfort besides, from whom after she was departed, she not satisfied with the former sight of her dear father, having respect neither to herself, nor to the press of the people and multitude that were about him, suddenly turned back again, and ran to him as before, took him about the neck, and divers times together most lovingly kissed him, and at last with a full heavy heart was fain to depart from him; the beholding whereof was to many of them that were present thereat so lamentable, that it made them for very sorrow to mourn and weep.

So remained Sir Thomas More in the Tower more than a sevennight after his judgment. From whence the day before he suffered he sent his shirt of hair, not willing to have it seen, to my wife, his dearly beloved daughter, and a letter, written with a coal, contained in the foresaid book of his works, plainly expressing the fervent desire he had to suffer on the morrow in these words: "I cumber you, good Margaret, much, but I would be sorry if it should be any longer than to-morrow. For to-morrow is St. Thomas' even, and the Octave of St. Peter, and therefore to-morrow long I to go to God, that were a day very meet and convenient for me. And I never liked your manners better, than when you kissed me last. For I like when daughterly love, and dear charity hath no leisure to look to worldly courtesy."

And so upon the next morning, being Tuesday, St. Thomas' even, and the Octave of St. Peter in the year of our Lord God 1537, according as he in his letter the day before had wished, early in the morning came to him Sir Thomas Pope, his singular friend, on message from the King and his Council, that he should before nine of the clock in the same morning suffer death, and that therefore forthwith he should prepare himself thereto. "Mr. Pope," saith he, "for your good tidings I most heartily thank you. I have been always bounden much to the King's Highness for the benefits and honours which he hath still from time to time most bountifully heaped upon me, and yet more bounded I am to his Grace for putting me into this place, where I have had convenient time and space to have remembrance of my end, and so help me God most of all, Mr. Pope, am I bound to his Highness, that it pleased him so shortly to rid me of the miseries of this wretched world. And therefore will I not fail most earnestly to pray

SIR THOMAS MORE, in his 50th year

for his Grace both here, and also in another world." "The King's pleasure is further," quoth Mr. Pope, "that at your execution you shall not use many words." "Mr. Pope" (quoth he), "you do well that you give me warning of his Grace's pleasure. For otherwise had I purposed at that time somewhat to have spoken, but of no matter wherewith his Grace, or any other should have had cause to be offended. Nevetheless whatsoever I intend I am ready obediently to conform myself to his Grace's commandment. And I beseech you, good Mr. Pope, to be a mean unto his Highness, that my daughter Margaret may be present at my burial." "The King is well contented already" (quoth Mr. Pope) "that your wife, children, and other friends shall have free liberty to be present thereat." "O how much beholden," then said Sir Thomas More, "am I to his Grace, that unto my poor burial vouchsafeth to have so gracious consideration." Wherewithal Mr. Pope taking his leave of him could not refrain from weeping, which Sir Thomas More perceiving, comforted him in this wise, "Quiet yourself, good Mr. Pope, and be not discomforted. For I trust that we shall once in heaven see each other full merrily, where we shall be sure to live and love together in joyful bliss eternally."

Upon whose departure Sir Thomas More, as one that had been invited to a solemn feast, changed himself into his best apparel; which Mr. Lieutenant espying, advised him to put it off, saying, That he that should have it was but a worthless fellow. "What Mr. Lieutenant" (quoth he), "shall I account him a worthless fellow, that will do me this day so singular a benefit? Nay, I assure you, were it cloth of gold I would account it well bestowed on him, as St. Cyprian did, who gave his executioner thirty pieces of gold." And albeit at length, through Mr. Lieutenant's persuasions, he altered his apparel, yet, after the example of that holy martyr St. Cyprian, did he of that little money that was left him, send one angel of gold to his executioner.

And so was he brought by Mr. Lieutenant out of the Tower, and from thence led towards the place of execution, where going up the scaffold, which was so weak that it was ready to fall, he said to Mr. Lieutenant, "I pray you, I pray you, Mr. Lieutenant, see me safe up, and for my coming down let me shift for myself." Then desired he all the people thereabouts to pray for him, and to bear witness with him, that he should then suffer death in and for the faith of the holy Catholic Church, which done he kneeled down, and after his prayers said, he turned to the executioner, and with a cheerful countenance spake unto him. "Pluck up thy spirits, man, and be not afraid to do thine office, my neck is very short. Take heed therefore thou shoot not awry for saving thine honesty."

So passed Sir Thomas More out of this world to God upon the very same day in which himself had most desired. Soon after whose death came intelligence thereof to the Emperor Charles, whereupon he sent for Sir Thomas Eliott, our English Ambassador, and said unto him, "My Lord Ambassador, we understand that the King your master hath put his faithful servant and grave wise councillor Sir Thomas More to death." Whereunto Sir Thomas Eliott answered, that he understood nothing thereof. "Well," said the Emperor, "it is very true, and this will we say, that if we had been master of such a servant, of whose doings ourselves have had these many years no small experience, we would rather have lost the best city of our dominions, than have lost such a worthy councillor." Which matter was by Sir Thomas Eliott to myself, to my wife, to Mr. Clement and his wife, to Mr. John Haywood and his wife, and divers others of his friends accordingly reported.